Jamaica

Michael Capek

🌿 Carolrhoda Books, Inc. / Minneapolis

Photo Acknowledgments

Photos, maps, and artworks are used courtesy of: John Erste, pp. 1, 2–3, 10–11, 21, 25, 27 (bottom), 36, 37; © Stephen Graham Photography, pp. 4, 14, 18 (top), 26 (left), 38; Laura Westlund, pp. 4–5, 23; © Robert Fried/Robert Fried Photography, pp. 6, 7 (top), 8, 31, 33 (bottom); **Photo Network:** (© Mark Sherman) p. 7 (bottom), (© Todd Powell) pp. 15 (bottom), 16, (© Jeff Greenberg) p. 20; Jamaica Tourist Board, pp. 9, 10, 24, 34, 35; **Visuals Unlimited:** (© Jeff Greenberg) pp. 12, 39, 45, (© Max & Bea Hunn) p. 44; Jim Simondet, p. 13; © Buddy Mays/Travel Stock Photography, pp. 15 (top), 26 (right), 33 (top); **Bruce Coleman, Inc.:** (© Guido Cozzi) pp. 17, 22–23, (© Tony Arruza) pp. 18 (bottom), 40, (© Elisa Leonelli) pp. 41, 43; © John and Penny Hubley, from the title *Jamaican Village*, A & C Black (Publishers) Limited, London, p. 19; Astor, Lenox, and Tilden Foundations, New York Public Library Rare Book Division, p. 27 (top); **©Trip:** (D. Saunders) p. 28, (R. Graham) p. 29; © W. Lynn Seldon, Jr., pp. 30, 42 (both); © Joan Iaconetti, p. 32. Cover photo © Stephen Graham Photography.

Carolrhoda Books, Inc.
c/o The Lerner Publishing Group
241 First Avenue North
Minneapolis, Minnesota 55401 U.S.A.

Website address: www. lernerbooks.com

Words in **bold type** are explained in a glossary that begins on page 46.

Library of Congress Cataloging-in-Publication Data

Capek, Michael
    Jamaica / by Michael Capek.
    p. cm. — (A ticket to)
    Includes bibliographical references and index.
    Summary: A brief introduction to the geography, culture, and people of Jamaica
    ISBN 1-57505-137-0 (lib. bdg. : alk. paper)
    1. Jamaica — Juvenile literature. [1. Jamaica.] I. Title. II. Series.
F1868.2.C37   1999
972.92—dc21   98—34185

Manufactured in the United States of America
1 2 3 4 5 6 – JR – 04 03 02 01 00 99

Contents

A sandy, white Jamaican beach meets the turquoise water of the Caribbean Sea.

Welcome!

The **island** of Jamaica sits in the part of the Atlantic Ocean called the Caribbean Sea.

It is easy to spot Jamaica on a **map.** Find the island of Cuba. It looks like a big dolphin. Can you find the island that sits to the south? You have found the island of Jamaica!

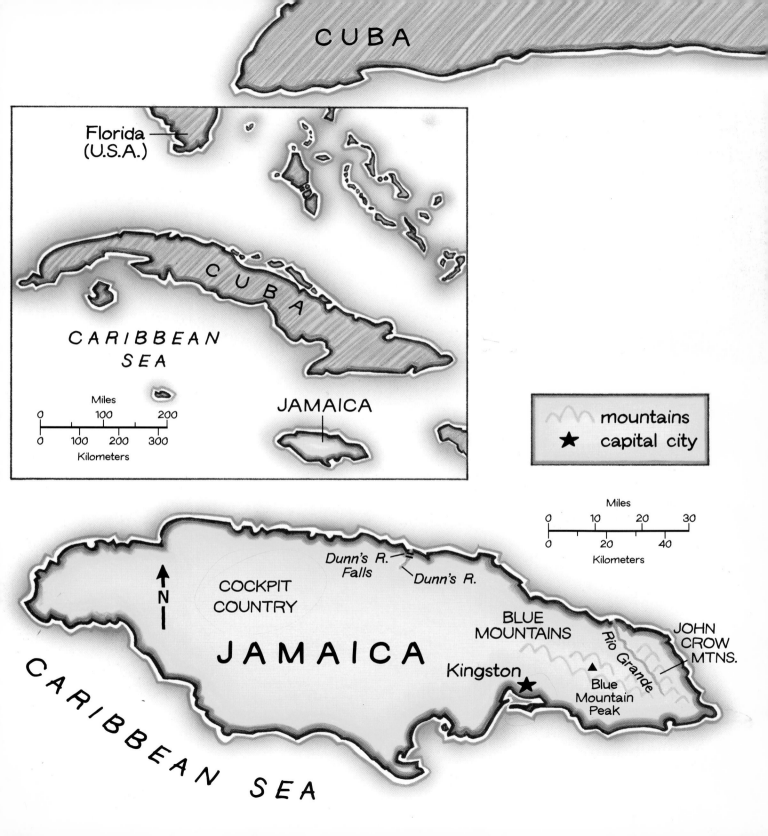

CUBA

Florida
(U.S.A.)

C U B A

CARIBBEAN
SEA

JAMAICA

Miles
0   100   200
0   100   200   300
Kilometers

⌢⌢⌢ mountains
★ capital city

Miles
0   10   20   30
0   20   40
Kilometers

COCKPIT
COUNTRY

Dunn's R.
Falls
Dunn's R.

BLUE
MOUNTAINS

JOHN
CROW
MTNS.

Rio Grande

J A M A I C A

N

Kingston
★
Blue
Mountain
Peak

C A R I B B E A N   S E A

Colorful coral lies beneath the waves off Jamaica's coast.

Wet and Wild

Jamaicans find water all across the island. Lots of rain falls in Jamaica each year. Rivers and creeks cut through the island. Many waterways plunge down slopes to waterfalls where kids love to splash.

Crocodiles float in the water, too. They swim next to boats where people might feed the crocodiles snacks. But watch your toes! Those teeth are sharp.

Dunn's River Falls is a cool spot for tourists and locals.

The American crocodile lives in many Jamaican rivers.

A small house perches in Jamaica's Blue Mountains.

Across the Island

Sandy beaches spread around most of
Jamaica. But in some spots, the Caribbean
Sea meets high cliffs. Fishing boats steer
into the **ports** on the island's coast.

Flat plains separate the coast from Jamaica's **mountain ranges.** The Blue Mountains rise on the eastern side of the island. Jamaica's tallest **mountain,** Blue Mountain Peak, pokes into the clouds. In the west, Cockpit Country has lots of hills and valleys.

Bumpy, pitted Cockpit Country is too hilly for farms. Almost no one lives there.

Warm Weather

If you go to Jamaica, bring your shorts and T-shirts! Jamaica has a **tropical climate.** That means the weather is hot and humid (wet). Banana plants and

The sun shines a lot on Jamaica.

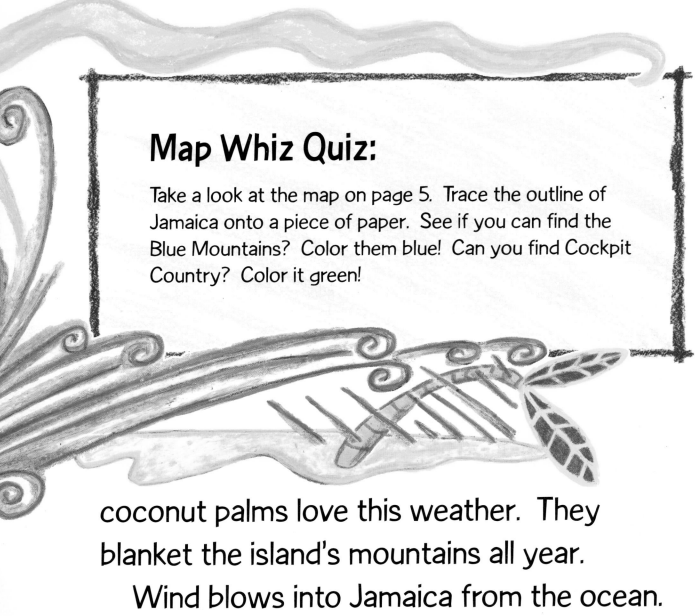

Map Whiz Quiz:

Take a look at the map on page 5. Trace the outline of Jamaica onto a piece of paper. See if you can find the Blue Mountains? Color them blue! Can you find Cockpit Country? Color it green!

coconut palms love this weather. They blanket the island's mountains all year.

Wind blows into Jamaica from the ocean. Jamaicans call the wind the Doctor Breeze. It makes people feel better on hot days.

This house once belonged to a slave owner. These days it is a museum!

Early Days

For hundreds of years, only the Arawak Indians lived in Jamaica. Spaniards arrived in the 1500s and forced the Arawak to work in the fields. When many Arawak died, the Spaniards brought Africans to work as slaves. In the 1600s, the British took over Jamaica.

They brought more people from Africa.
Some slaves escaped. Many joined the
Maroons, a group of former slaves who lived
in Jamaica's hills and mountains. The
Maroons fought against the slaveholders
until 1834, when the British freed the slaves.

Jamaica's flag has three colors. Green stands for Jamaica's farms. Black stands for the country's past. Yellow stands for sunshine.

The Jamaicans

This woman has come to Jamaica to visit her friend. Long ago his relatives were newcomers, too.

A favorite Jamaican saying is, "Out of many, one people." That is because the people who live on the island are proud to be Jamaicans. Most Jamaicans trace their

Where do you think these Jamaican boys' relatives came from?

families to Africa. Some have relatives from Europe or Asia. Lots of Jamaicans have relatives from two or more **continents.**

15

Big City

Kingston, Jamaica's **capital,** rests on the southern coast near the Blue Mountains.

Kingston has a beautiful natural harbor.

About one out of three Jamaicans lives in this city. Huge ships arrive in a port. Taxis, buses, and people crowd the roads. On every corner, music blares from radios. Families live in brightly painted apartment houses that squeeze next to restaurants, churches, and shops. Pet pigs, cats, and dogs roam the streets. Imagine that!

Kingston has many different neighborhoods. This one is busy!

Family Ties

A mother and her children relax in their backyard (below). This aunt will help to raise her baby niece (right).

In Jamaica, families are big! Moms and dads often have three or more kids. Aunts, uncles, grandmas, and grandpas usually live nearby. Family members like to help each other out. Moms are in charge

Some Jamaican kids take jobs to help their families with money. This boy runs errands in his own cart.

of raising their kids, but grandmas and aunts pitch in. Lots of kids are taken care of by "aunties" who are not related. These aunties are good friends of the family.

Shopping

Most Jamaican families live in the countryside. On tiny farms they grow yams (which are like potatoes),

Jamaican shoppers have many choices in this open-air market.

breadfruit (a type of fruit), beans, and other foods. Yum! Farmers sell their extra food at open-air markets in towns.

Some merchants spread their goods on the sidewalk. They set high prices. Shoppers **bargain** to get a good deal. That is part of the fun!

Patois

English is Jamaica's official language. In school, kids speak English. But on the streets and at home, most Jamaicans speak a kind of English called **patois.** Patois sounds like English spoken with a Jamaican accent.

Some patois words come from Arawak, French, Spanish, or African languages. Do you think Jamaicans use patois on the phone?

Dear Holly,

Jamaica is like a warm, green garden. This morning was sunny. We walked in a field full of huge golden butterflies bigger than my hand. Later it began to rain. Auntie found a giant banana leaf to use as an umbrella!

Walk Good! (That is how Jamaicans say good-bye.)

Grace

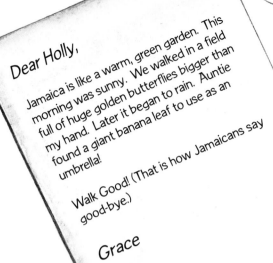

Here are some patois expressions. Try them out on your friends. Can they understand you?

Boonoonoonoos   beautiful

Cool runnings   greetings

Nyam   eat

Tenky   thank you

23

Celebrate

Jamaicans love to celebrate! Music festivals bring fans together. Famous musicians and beginners perform.

Dancers wear crazy costumes for Jonkonnu—a festival that dates back to the days of slavery.

Some celebrations mark religious holidays. Jonkonnu is a favorite Christmas **tradition.** To celebrate, folks wear masks as they dance, drum, and sing in village streets. The outfits are wild! One person wears a mixed-up costume with the tusks of a wild boar, a sword, and a cow's tail. Other merrymakers might dress up like brides or devils.

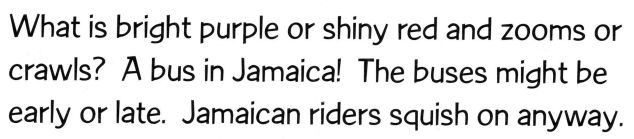

When Jamaicans want to go somewhere, they might ride a bike (above) *or hop onto a raft* (right).

Getting There

What is bright purple or shiny red and zooms or crawls? A bus in Jamaica! The buses might be early or late. Jamaican riders squish on anyway.

Other Jamaicans drift on rafts. Before you get on, take off your shoes. The rafts get pretty wet. Watch out for the rapids!

Pirates

Long ago pirates such as these two sailed the Caribbean Sea. They stole treasure from other ships. Some even stole sailing ships from their victims. Where did pirates hide out? Jamaica! These days ships bring tourists and goods to the island instead of stolen treasure.

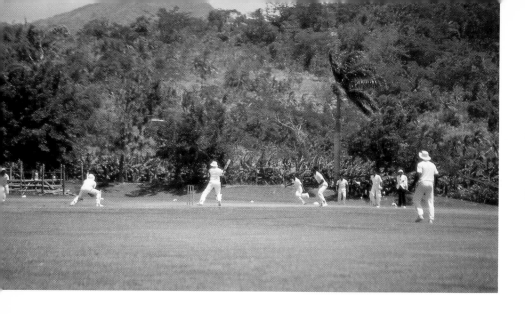

Jamaican cricket teams play against teams from other Caribbean islands.

Game Time

Wack! A ball goes flying, and the crowd goes wild. Fans are cheering, singing, dancing, and drumming. What is going on? You are at a cricket game in Jamaica! Cricket is a little bit like baseball. It is Jamaica's favorite team sport. Running is a popular activity, too. Jamaican athletes have won Olympic medals for their speed!

Jamaicans love to play dominoes.
Youngsters and old folks alike can pit their
wits against each other in this game.

*A young cricket
player swings hard
at an incoming ball.*

This Jamaican student is ready for the schoolday to begin.

Time for School

Jamaican kids start school when they turn six years old. They learn to read, to write, and to do math. In class, students do not speak patois. They speak English.

Jamaican schools are crowded. Kids have to share books and desks. In fact, so many kids go to school that Jamaica holds two schooldays every day. Half of the students go to school in the morning. The other half go in the afternoon!

A group of students gather in their classroom.

These elementary-school girls wear uniforms. Does your school require uniforms?

All Dressed Up

It is so hot in Jamaica that lots of kids wear swimsuits or shorts all year. On schooldays, students put on tidy uniforms. Girls wear skirts or jumpers. Boys dress in pants and matching jackets. Jamaican kids wear clean

This woman's pale kerchief will keep her head cool in the hot sun (left). A man wears a *floppy hat called a tam* (below).

white shirts under their uniforms.

Most grown-ups do not wear uniforms. Jamaican men usually wear pants and shirts. Women choose comfortable dresses.

Art

This artist has carved his own face in wood.

Jamaican artists carve beautiful wooden sculptures of people and nature scenes. Others use bright paints to make small pictures or huge murals (large paintings on walls or on ceilings). Many Jamaican artists

like their work to reflect their African
heritage, but they also like to show that
they are Jamaicans.

*You might
find Jamaican
paintings for
sale on the
street or
hanging in
one of the
country's
museums.*

Dub Poetry

Jamaicans love to watch poets perform.
Some dub poets tell old Jamaican **folktales.**

Anancy!

Some dub poets tell stories
about Anancy, a magic spider.
He tricks other animals who
brag or who think that they are
more clever than he is. Anancy
stories came to
Jamaica from Africa
with the slaves.

Others recite new poems about hard times or happy events.

These poets speak in patois. With its strong rhythms, dub poetry is a little bit like rap music. Some dub poets have music playing in the background. Huge crowds come to watch dub poets perform. They do not just watch! The fans shout, clap, and drum along with the poet.

Reggae Beat

Put together musicians banging drums, strumming electric guitars, and singing songs written in patois. That is reggae— Jamaica's favorite kind of music!

A man plays his guitar and sings for customers at a small restaurant.

Bob Marley

Bob Marley was Jamaica's most famous reggae performer. The house where he once lived has been made into a popular museum. A statue of the singer greets visitors outside.

Fans across the world love this Jamaican music. It is like rock and roll with an island flavor. Most reggae songs are about peace, love, or cooperation.

These Christian women have just been to church. Does your family dress up for a weekly religious service?

Faith

Most Jamaicans are Christians. The Spanish and British slave owners shared their religion with their African slaves. Many Jamaicans follow religions with African roots. Some folks combine belief systems.

The shaggy hair of Rastafarians is supposed to look like the mane of the lion, a Rasta symbol.

Some Jamaicans started a religion called Rastafarianism. Rastafarians are easy to spot! That is because they wear their hair in long, thick twists called dreadlocks.

Rastafarians are vegetarians, which means that they do not eat meat. And they believe in peace.

A woman serves herself some food (left) *—it smells good! Akee* (above) *is Jamaica's favorite fruit. When it is ripe, the fruit splits open to show three shiny, black seeds.*

Barbecue Time

Nyam! Remember that word? It is patois for *eat.*

Long-ago Jamaicans came up with a way to cook what they called *barbacoa.* They covered meat with a spicy sauce and roasted it over an open fire. The fires were built in holes in the ground.

These days folks say barbecue, and most Jamaicans cook meat on grills instead of in open pits. In Jamaican cities and towns, it is easy to find a barbecue stall. Look for the thick smoke and follow your nose. Yum!

Jamaicans love a kind of barbecue called jerk. The word jerk *stands for a special blend of spices and herbs that flavors the meat.*

43

New Words to Learn

bargain: A talk between a buyer and a seller about the cost of an item. Bargaining ends when both sides agree on a price.

capital: A city where the government is located.

continent: One of the seven great divisions of land on the globe.

folktale: A timeless story told by word of mouth from grandparent to parent to child. Many folktales have been written down in books.

A farmworker uses a large knife to cut stalks of sugarcane, which will be made into table sugar.

Dressed in leaves, a coconut seller slices up his goods for customers to taste.

island: A piece of land surrounded by water.

map: A drawing or chart of all or part of the earth or sky.

mountain range: A series, or group, of **mountains**—the parts of the earth's surface that rise high into the sky.

patois: A form of English that also includes non-English words.

port: A safe area on the shore of a body of water where ships can load and unload goods.

tradition: A way of doing things—such as preparing a meal, celebrating a holiday, or making a living—that a group of people practice.

tropical climate: A yearly weather condition that is usually hot and in which lots of rain falls every year.

New Words to Say

akee	AH-kee
Anancy	ah-NAHN-see
Arawak	AIR-uh-wahk
barbacoa	bar-buh-COH-ah
barbecue	BAR-buh-kyoo
boonoonoonoose	boo-NOO-noo-noose
Caribbean Sea	cair-uh-BEE-uhn SEE
cool runnings	KOOL RON-nings
Jamaica	jah-MAY-kah
nyam	NEE-yahm
patois	PAT-wah
Rastafarian	rahs-tah-FAHR-ee-ahn
reggae	REH-gay
tenky	TAIN-kee

More Books to Read

Benitez, Mirna and Dorothea Sierra. *How Spider Tricked Snake.* Milwaukee: Raintree/Steck Vaughn, 1990.

Brownlie, Alison. *Jamaica.* Milwaukee: Raintree/Steck Vaughn, 1998.

Burgie, Irving. *Caribbean Carnival: Songs of the West Indies .* New York: William Morrow & Company, Inc., 1992.

Hausman, Gerald. *Doctor Bird: Three Lookin' Up Tales from Jamaica.* New York: Philomel Books, 1998.

Hubley, John and Penny Hubley. *A Family in Jamaica.* Minneapolis: Lerner Publications Company, 1985.

Pluckrose, Henry Arthur. *Picture Jamaica.* Chicago: Franklin Watts, 1998.

Temple, Frances. *Tiger Soup: An Anansi Story from Jamaica.* New York: Orchard Books, 1994.

Thompson, Julie and Brownie MacIntosh. *A Pirate's Life for Me!: A Day aboard a Pirate Ship.* Watertown, MA: Charlesbridge Publishing, 1996.

New Words to Find